BEING BUSY IS NOT ALWAYS PRODUCTIVE

DEEPAK GUPTA

Contents

Master Acknowledgement

I don't know what I should say to my beloved readers. I'm not that fine at writing the acknowledgement of my books, but I can say **appreciation is much better than earning money.** I want to thank every reader who purchased my books with their precious money. My cells thank every reader a million times. Before I'm a writer, I'm a reader, a human, and an observer. I want to clarify; we all possess a kind of productivity to accomplish our work. We all specialize in doing some work. In our opinion, we all should do the work in which our productivity is high & stop looking for the work that doesn't belong to us. Success doesn't overflow overnight. Slow and steady win the race. I had a little to say before I awakened my vision. Burn your ego if you want to learn something new every day. People and books have something distinctive to offer the world. I have emerged from my uniqueness right now. I want to say a significant lesson, never feel worthless if no one appreciates you. Don't ever feel useless because we can overcome failure but can't overcome the self-made failure. ***If anyone wants to take any kind of interview, may be online, or to ask some questions, then I welcome all the readers, Youtubers, Bloggers, Artists, and editors.*** Work on your art because the work we love can never disappoint us in any point in time.

With Love & Respect
Deepak Gupta

Stop Here And Absorb

'If we want to learn from a mother, we should become her child and if we want to learn from the child, we should become his mother.'

Burn your ego before proceeding to learn something great from this book. Our education and learning are the process but, not the destination. **Don't go ahead of humanity; the ego lies there.** We ignore uncomplicated lessons in life that become the hardest lessons in the end. Before we learn tough, we should learn simple lessons in life.

Prologue

You know why people fail because they use their right energy in the wrong place. They use their energy at a place where they can't even judge how much capability they have to accomplish the right tasks. People fail at the wrong tasks and get afraid to do the right tasks in life. **Time has nothing to do with productivity.** We have been seeing people who succeeded without efforts, but we forget to understand their passion at the right place. Time matters when we do significant things in our lives. Productivity and right activities go together. Productivity always adds something new to your life progress. Many people work for the full day and get tired, while there are also some people who work for the whole day and don't feel tired for a second. Why, because those people get the right satisfaction from their work. It may be anything like writing, painting, cooking, dressing, or it may be any work they love to do. There's nothing static we should do to increase our productivity. One work may tempt & look good to us, but may look boring to someone.

The real risk to our lives lies in our time span. We study for the whole life to succeed. Everyone studies but only a few achieve success in real. Why, because our education system pushes all of us into a single field. We are pushed to do the work we don't even love. If we tell engineers to solve tax problems, they will fall out. Being busy is not always a sign of productivity. ***Some people think in the bathroom, while some don't even work in the workplace.*** We choose what is easy, not what is necessary. Some day we don't have the choice to do what we really love. Choosing the right path and career is really tough these days. Everyone has aspirations from us, but we can't fulfil the aspirations of everyone. We should decide what we can do with passion and productivity. We should choose the work for which we don't feel tired for our whole life. ***We are not tired; we are just in the wrong place, trying to dig out some productivity. Nothing works there.***

Education is significant, but learning in life is a new experience. We study for the whole life to get the job. Do we all have the same aspirations and goals to get the job? No, we don't have that. We are attracted to money than to do our job with the best productivity. We are attracted by education to earn money and make our productivity a new sense of business. We work for money than to think about how it will affect our life.

Our real risk is, we study for the whole time and still feel unproductive. A little span of time decides our long span of time. If we talk about any of the great personalities like Albert Einstein or Charles Dickens, they remember the law of productivity. They never ran behind success; they ran behind the work in which their productivity was high. **Everyone has a role to play. No one can replace anyone.** We are allowed to appreciate everyone contributing their valuable productivity to this world. Businesses and jobs both are art if these tasks go with the right person. No one would ever tell us to do productive tasks in the long run. We all are fascinated by money, not the position. If someone is earning from that profession, then I can also earn. No, that attitude is wrong. He is earning well because he chose a field that increases his productivity. ***Your choice is your real implementation of time. Choose your work than running behind money all the time. Money is the by-product of passion.***

'We study for 20 years and get failed. Don't we think we really need to think about this? How we can get failed even we study for a long time. Because we focus on our education only, but learning begins when we start to implement our ideas with our productivity. ***Don't ever confuse education with learning.'***

CHAPTER ONE

LIFE IS NOT THE COIN

'Life is not the coin. It has lessons with numbers on the dice. Every time we throw it; we learn something different and new. It depends on us how we use it better in our life.'

Confucius said, our greatest glory is not in never falling, but in rising every time we fall. We all have turning points in our lives. Suppose a person works for a company, & one day the employer fired him with some bullshit excuse. What will the person do? Our life should get changed positively even with other people. People are good when we appreciate them. A person shouldn't waste his life working for others. People's productivity rises in the field they never wanted to choose. How well companies play to lure us to do anything. We all have our turning points in life when we get fed up with luxury, money, and society. We want to spend quality time with our loved ones. Our quality time is the time in which we have something great to learn & to get love in the right way.

Money increases with time but productivity should increase exponentially with time. Start your day with recognition.

In my opinion, our life goes straight but with some hustle-bustle. When we face real problems, we get to know our real capability to take the right decisions. ***People die young and stay unhappy for their own reason.*** Some cover designers make brilliant covers in a few minutes because they have mastered it by investing their time. ***Master your skills with a rapid increase in productivity.*** We can achieve the same productivity in a year that people achieve in 20 years. Time span has nothing to do with productivity. We should know our turning points in life to get the opportunity to learn and understand human behaviour.

Productivity should be like a thick rope. First, it should be 1x, then 2x 1x the 2x 2x 1x, and so on. I learned my vision well in the last year; even I have been writing since 2015. ***If you really want to make anything work in your life, start value the progress before someone can do it for you.*** Our turning point decides whether we are productive or not.

CHAPTER TWO

YOU AREN'T UNIQUE. WE ARE ALL UNIQUE

Do you feel like procrastinating on tasks the whole day? Do you feel like wasting your time & still doing it, and then rush to achieve the tasks in the least time? Probably the answer is yes, because humans are born with attributes and laziness. There's no shame in it. You aren't unique. We all are unique. We ruin our day when we have nothing productive to make our day better. There are two different time dimensions to achieve our goals, may be in the morning or at night. Both times are good, but it depends on how flexible and productive we are at that time. Waiting for the right time & utilising it, both are different stories.

Our morning productivity gets high when we have sound sleep at night, but how we use our mind well in that time, makes our whole day. If we don't eat breakfast, we feel bad for the whole day because we think we have lost something good from our meal. Just like food, our minds need productive tasks when it gets active, otherwise it would get indulge and try to get busy in useless activities. Decide your task for the next day before you sleep, and your mind will alarm you again and again and will prevent your mind from getting busy in the wrong tasks.

We should accomplish our tasks in the morning than waiting for some feasible time. I have big reasons for this lesson.First, as our morning productivity is high, we try and make it our best work. We should know what our real standard is and how far and best we can do in our work. **Second,** our mind also gets the unique ability to get appreciated if we do it early than procrastinate it for the whole day. After applying, you will feel well for the whole day and try to make yourself productive & creative for the remaining day. I tried this in my everyday routine many times and trust me; this will make your personality happy and a nice person. You will never feel frustrated or even sad for a moment. For the whole day, our brain will signal to ourselves to get appreciated & direction to work better for the time ahead.

A work done before time gives sense of satisfaction and more energy; but a work done after the desired time loses the satisfaction level & brings stress in our life. Always try to accomplish your work before time.

Our morning productivity and work decide our whole day's happiness and satisfaction.

CHAPTER THREE

DON'T CONFUSE YOURSELF WITH EDUCATION AND LEARNING

We study hard, still less educated people win by their art, how?What's the real scenario going on? We have a simple answer to this, and we know this comes to your mind every day.

If you try to serve the society and get appreciated, you will never get tired. People are hungry for appreciation than looking for money. We are talking about real people. Many Youtubers, film stars, writers, and other professionals get successful even if they don't have education at such a higher level. We are saying it again. Don't confuse education with learning. There are smart minds wandering in the world. Practicality of life with passion and art are famous these days, but don't think it as a short cut to get fame. *In a world where everyone wants to become a billionaire but no one ever sits to think, why?* Why do we really need so much money? ***Money can't bring happiness. The ways we spend & live money bring happiness to our life.***

The scenario has changed in the 21st century where everyone is the king of their own kingdom, and no one wants to listen to anyone and that's how we lose ourselves in the journey. **Education is significant, but its implementation is much significant than that. Academic education is like making a giant machine without testing it even for one time.** Less education may be okay, but less learning is deadly. People who are getting success are the ones who know to learn better with education. Be the man of virtues, productivity, and learning than to look for education only. Education leads to learning, but less education has nothing to do with it.

Learning can be increased by testing what we get from our education. Test yourself without worrying about results. ***Don't get busy with the wrong tasks. Do it late, but make it right and absolutely accurate.***

Success isn't attached to money & fame but to the goals. Goals design the path of success to get satisfaction from everyday work.

CHAPTER FOUR

NO, LIFE DOESN'T WORK LIKE THAT

Some people earn millions in a day while some don't even earn one crore in their whole life. It really makes sense to think again, that money has nothing to do with time. Everything is all about enthusiasm, productivity, passion, and truth.

If you want to earn a lot of money, first, sharpen your skills in an exponential way than to worry about money initially. It's simple to say and hard to implement. It's like working hard presently and leaving our success in the hands of the future. I know it's hard. We can't stop our expenses at any time. We can't stop the clock. Money earning is not bad, but if we are not learning anything new while moving ahead in life then we would die with that money only. Like our productivity, your money should have exponential growth. We earn millions throughout our life, then what? Life is better when we leave something creative at the end to remember. ***The wrong scenario is wandering around people that people remind us for money. No, life doesn't work like that. People like us for what we do, not about how much we earn.*** According to the society's opinion, **Jeff Bezos**, CEO of Amazon, is the greatest person of all time. He's not great for his money, but for the innovative ideas of his company.

We all have the chance to double our money the last day of our life, but if we face death, we would try to double our productivity and relationship because nothing goes with us. ***Live like you would die today. Treat your sleep like death. Accomplish every task before you sleep. That's the only way to revive the everyday life.***

'Money should be secondary when it becomes primary.'

CHAPTER FIVE

A Golden Method to Remember Everything

We make mistakes, learn, and leave them in the same place. That's human behaviour. I have a practical concept to share with you. ***Your today is not just today; it's the cumulative efforts of all your days. We live all past days to see today.*** We fight a big journey to see today. Today should be remembered for something beautiful than to waste it somewhere else.

We say it cumulative life because today is the composition of all our old days. Whatever we learned; we should implement it better to make our today. Our lessons are useless if we repeat the same mistakes. If you gave 100 percent in the past, then today is the day to give your 200 percent, and who decides this, you only. We all have excuses for something, but no one gets remembered for their excuses. I love to go through challenges, and you should do. Every lesson we repeat we lose one day, and so on. How would you feel when you get to know & understand that you wasted your days for nothing? It feels bad, but you can still revive to learn from your cumulative precious life.

Make your life understandable than make it modern. ***Flowers glow when roots grow from inside. Do what we can remind for long and learn from it.***

Productivity is the accumulation of understanding the mistakes of all cumulative past days. Repeating the mistakes is like repeating the days.

CHAPTER SIX

Don't ever Switch

We try everything in life but get succeeded in one passion at a time. Those who put their legs in two boats get drowned forever. Don't ever try to switch between the various tasks; otherwise, your mind will get confused. To increase your productivity, put yourself in one work and do it continuously. The day will surely come when you understand the power of one passion at a time. The rest of our works is our temptation to earn money or get successful.

There's always one key for a lock. If you try to unlock everything, nothing will open. We all have the keys, and our real task is to find the real lock. May be someone's earning tempts you to join some sector, but then you realise you failed because you went for something wrong because of other reasons than to test your real productivity. I see a lot of professions to work in, but not everything belongs to us. **Do one at a time and put five times energy of passion in it.** You will surely get the results. I repeat, don't jump or switch between goals.

One lock has one key, and the rest are just illusions and temptations of our minds. Teach yourself and stop wasting time on the wrong art of life.

Our minds are infinite, but they can handle similar related information in infinite ways. If we ask our minds to choose between the two tasks, they get confused because they need relevant related information to take decisions. Multiple unrelated situations confuse our minds to take better decisions. Clear your mind and help it work in the right direction.

CHAPTER SEVEN

INVEST YOUR ENERGY THAN USING IT

We believe a person should invest his energy than using it. Yes, both are much different. When we put our energy in the right place, we get more energetic. Only in the wrong tasks, we get tired after a time. You can be sad, but you can't get tired when you achieve the right goals.

Our energy gets doubled for the right art of life. If something is not giving you a sense of happiness, peace and accomplishments, then you are doing it wrong. In the century of stress, always, be the person of energy. It's the real secret to attract people. Do you have something to talk about? Then talk about it well. **Build your confidence, and people will listen to you.** Like I talked about cumulative life, if we accumulate negative vibes every day, we will reach the path of depression. A little happiness reduces much depression in our lives.

I feel like one unit of happiness can reduce ten units of depression. I know how I can measure happiness, but we do it daily and make it countable like to say to others, I was in depression for three days, but never make the efforts and appreciate to count the happiness of the rest of our life. Be the cause of someone's happiness and find the reason for your depression.

When we do the work we love, we become more energetic. Our body and mind are simple units. They go in the line where we push consistently. If we push them in an energetic line, they become more energetic & passionate to do more & more stress-free work.

'Make it relevant before making it easy.'

CHAPTER EIGHT

THEORY AND PRACTICAL OF PRODUCTIVITY

The world grows from practical experience to theories, not from theories to practical. We read everything, but somewhere our approach to applying ideas is wrong. We read, then we learn to apply. The world has changed a lot. I was also confused when I saw something and tried to apply. No, that's wrong. You have your capabilities and art. Your experience is different from mine. We all see our world differently. We all see the moon but from our own space. May be the bright star you see, looks dull to me. ***As I said in my book, The Power of Universe, your sun will rise when your sky appears blue.***

Books are born with ideas. The theories we all read, emerged and were written after practical experience. If we don't look around the world and read the theories only then, we will never be able to grow well. ***Maybe you have a weird idea, but it should be unique. Your ideas stand uniquely in the crowd. Open your vision to see the world differently.*** People teach us to read the theories, then tell us to make it practical. No, absolutely no. Try it yourself first. Most of the philosophers like Chanakya, Confucius, Martin Luther King, and many more experienced the world first and wrote about it later. If we learn theories every time, we will learn what had already been discovered by someone. It's good to learn, but if nothing new grows with our vision, then there's some problem.

Our productivity rises with time in the presence of practical experience. The combination of theories and practical experience are the best combination. Read, apply, and then believe it.

Wrong: Theories to Practical

Right: Practical to Theories.

'Productivity is nothing but the real mindset to believe own ideas and make it happen.'

CHAPTER NINE

OLD IS ALWAYS GOLD: LEARNING FROM ANCIENT ART

Old is gold. Someone said it right. The value of ancient things is always greater than new things. If you want to possess some attributes, then accept the terms of ancient rules. Ancient things are popular for their stable art and happiness. Every time we look, we find something different to learn. A personality should be like ancient gold. Every time people see you; they learn something good from you. In the 21st century, people want innovation with everything. We need to learn that we should always have something great to offer to people, and they will appreciate us for a long time.

Most of the relationships go for a long time because some people grow with real art but don't change for which they were known by people. People will forget us if we change ourselves completely. If people know you for happiness, always be the same for those attributes. We buy gold because it doesn't change over time and its value increases with time. Productivity and time both possess the same art. They both should increase exponentially. Once someone asked me who I am, my answer was simple. We are what we do alone. We are what we remain after removing the profession from our lives. Readers know me for my artistic books, that's my profession, but who knows me in real life, people who are still with me. Your productivity will get double if you see opportunities within the trouble. Don't ever focus too much on problems, but change your way to look at it. The answer lies in the question. It's better to search for where it lies.

Five people can do better publicity than individuals alone. That's productivity. ***You have to be the leader who leads people in the right way. If you look for the benefit of everyone, you will lead the way easily. Don't ever focus on the wrong things.***

Not everyone is free. Some people are in prison while some become prisoners in their minds. Freedom is the real state of mind.

CHAPTER TEN

YOUR MIND IS A PARACHUTE. OPEN IT WELL

If your mind wanders everywhere without your permission, then you need to learn this chapter seriously. If you want to go for productivity, your mind should never jump around everything. Money and overnight success can tempt us to do the tasks that don't even belong to us. Stop switching between the activities you do.

'Continuity is a matter of real productivity.'

A book is nothing but the disciplined and continuous efforts of a writer. A book can't be completed without the real dedication level of any writer. A writer has to write every day to accomplish the book. No matter how he feels & how well he writes. Remove money and overnight success from your mind and you will learn what you really love to do. Like there's a confused mind that reside in our body, it gets fascinated by anything that brings real comfort and luxury to our mind. Step out and think about what you actually are when you don't earn money. I keep my books short because time is valuable, whether it's yours or mine.

Learn better in a short time. People accomplish tasks, but the person who accomplishes tasks in a real reasonable time, is the person of productivity.

Whatever we do and whoever we meet, everyone has something special to give us to learn. Keep learning.

CHAPTER ELEVEN

HOW TO ACCEPT THE TRUTH

As we said, stay productive than being busy with your tasks. **People have so many things to learn, and they get confused with what they actually need to learn.** People can't identify what is true and what is false. What they should learn and what they should leave. The question is how to find the right truth to learn and make ourselves productive.

There are certain attributes you should learn about the truth. ***People don't accept the truth initially. They test it by themselves. They see the results and accept it later.*** If people find it right in their life, then it becomes the truth of their life. May be something feels like truth to you and false to me. It depends on our circumstances. There are two types of truth; first is the universal truth and the other is dynamic truth. We need learning the difference between both. As we all are in quarantine and at our homes, my wish you all are safe and most importantly, happy and at peace. The world is healing and that's our universal truth. The sky is clear and blue. Now the wind is warm but not polluted. How simple words change everything in life.

The truth has no expiry date. If you said it today and it's true, it would go on for long, no matter what. The God is truth and we all accept it. We all know the truth but get afraid to accept it. How harsh the truth is, accept it because one day we all have to. I'm a very fragile person who is always in search of peace and luxury comes in my life later. If there's peace in the middle of the road, you may find me there. To search for what I have learned till now, I have to go inside and wander in my real veins peacefully. Accept the truth, and you will find every time productive.

Humans have to accept the reality to find solutions to present situations. Our minds find answers when we accept the questions. It's as simple as that.

Epilogue

'If being busy is not always productive then what makes us productive and what's the real test to know about the real utilization of our life.'

The Real Test of Productivity: The uniform increment and exponential increment are both different. Priority is easy and can be achieved in the short term, but the latter can only be achieved in the long term. If your results have no long-term impact on your productivity, maybe you are doing it wrong. We work for a company for years and then get fired. People have the right to teach us but not to change our lives negatively. If you want to test your level of productivity, ask two questions!

First, is the work I'm doing having long term positive results in my life? **Second**, to see, will my art remain the same as I'm seeing it today? Do I really help myself to improve the level of my productivity? The real work never disappoints you in any case. Little, meaningful sentences can change our world & remember, little money can never trouble us.

Maybe you are busy, but what's the real outcome. To make yourself productive, think about what you will do after accomplishing it. ***Celebrate your accomplishments.*** We always feel appreciated for the right task. ***We can be wrong, but our aura and vibes don't say it wrong.*** The long-term results and achievements tell our utilisation of time and energy in our life.

About The Author

Deepak Gupta is pre-eminently known for writing plain sailing, meticulous, and pragmatic Self-Help books.

He's the author of **more than forty books** including **10 Principles to Beat Failure** that won **Google Best Choice 2018** & became **Top Seller on Google Play Store in 2019**. He has been garnering much acclaim for his **30 Minutes Read & 10 Principles Series**. Till now, he has received **490k+ readership & a lot of appreciation** from all over the world. He believes in writing & living best exceptional content from his subconscious mind. He loves to observe, absorb, and write on various social issues, inspirational truthful words, short stories, and heart whelming poetry. Also, he has travelled to many places in India like Manali, Rajasthan, Goa, Kolkata, Madhya Pradesh, Jammu, Dalhousie, and Mussoorie to bring descent originality in his work. He ***releases new short books every month*** to get readers to connect with the truth of life.

Deepak Gupta received his post-graduation degree from **Delhi School of Economics**. Also, when he's not writing, he can be found wandering on his **exquisite terrace garden**. He lives with his family in **Delhi, India**.

Keep in touch with Deepak via the web:

Instagram @authordeepakgupta

Facebook: facebook.com/authordeepakgupta

Twitter @authordeepakgup

9 798886 410235

Printed by Libri Plureos GmbH in Hamburg, Germany